## DATE DUE

| | | | |
|---|---|---|---|
| 6-06-19 | | | |
| | | | |
| | | | |
| | | | |
| | | | |
| | | | |
| | | | |
| | | | |
| | | | |
| | | | |
| | | | |
| | | | |

**CONTINENTS**

# Asia

Leila Merrell Foster

Heinemann Library
Chicago, Illinois

Designed by Joanna Hinton-Malivoire and Q2A Creative
Printed in China by South China Printing Company

10 09 08 07 06
10 9 8 7 6 5 4 3 2 1

New edition ISBN: 1-4034-8541-0 (hardcover)
                  1-4034-8549-6 (paperback)

**The Library of Congress has cataloged the first edition as follows:**
Foster, Leila Merrell.
        Asia / Leila Merrell Foster.
                p. cm. – (Continents)
        Includes bibliographical references and index.
        ISBN 1-57572-448-0
        1. Asia—Juvenile literature. [1. Asia.] I. Title. II. Continents (Chicago, Ill.)
DS5 .F67  2001
950–dc21                                                                00-011466

**Acknowledgments**
The publishers are grateful to the following for permission to reproduce copyright material: Tony Stone/Mike Surowiak p. 4; Getty Images/Photographer's Choice/Stuart Dee p. 7; Bruce Coleman Inc./J. Montgomery p. 9; Bruce Coleman Inc./Burnett H. Moody p. 11; Earth Scenes/Robert Kloepper p.13; Getty Images/Lonely Planet Images/Lee Foster p. 15; Tony Stone/Mickey Gibson p. 16; Bruce Coleman, Inc./M. Freeman p. 17; Bruce Coleman Inc./Lynn M.Stone p.18; Bruce Coleman Inc./K&K Ammann p. 19; Tony Stone/D.E. Cox p. 21; Tony Stone/Orion Press p. 22; Getty Images/Lonely Planet/Mark Daffey p. 24; Bruce Coleman, Inc./Carolos V. Causo p. 25; Tony Stone/Keren Su p. 27; Corbis/Glen Allison p. 28; Tony Stone/Chris Haigh p. 29.

Cover photograph of Asia, reproduced with permission of Science Photo Library/ Worldsat International and J. Knighton.

The publishers would like to thank Kathy Peltan, Keith Lye, and Nancy Harris for their assistance in the preparation of this book.

Every effort has been made to contact copyright holders of any material reproduced in this book. Any omissions will be rectified in subsequent printings if notice is given to the publisher.

> Some words are shown in bold, **like this**. You can find out what they mean by looking in the glossary.

# Contents

# Where is Asia?

There are seven continents. A continent is a very large area of land. Asia is the largest continent. The west of Asia is connected to the continent of Europe.

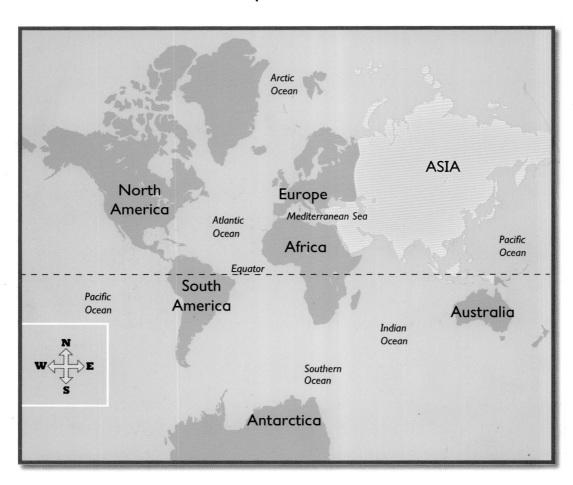

China is part
of the Far East.

▲ *The island of Hong Kong is close to China.*

The Mediterranean Sea is to the west of Asia.
The Pacific Ocean is to the east of Asia. The
countries on the Pacific coast are known as the
Far East. The area around the Mediterranean
Sea is part of the Middle East.

# Weather

The countries of Asia have many different **climates**. Above the **Arctic Circle**, the land stays frozen all year round. In central Asia, there are large **deserts**, where almost no rain falls.

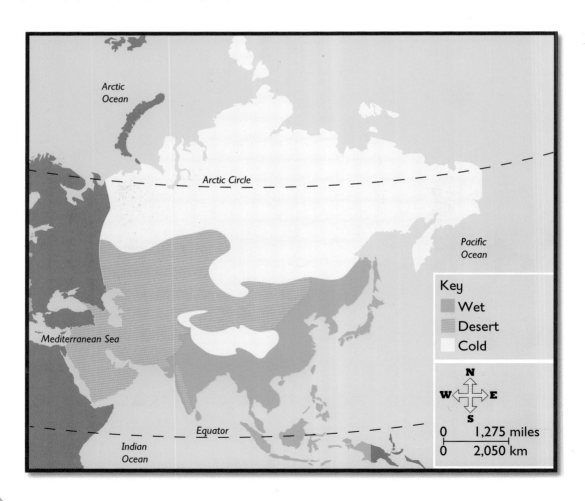

▲ *Rain forest in Southeast Asia.*

The **Equator** is an imaginary line around the center of Earth. Around the Equator, the weather is very hot. It rains every day in the **rain forests** of southern Asia. The weather is warm and sunny near the Mediterranean Sea.

# Mountains

Asia has many high mountain **ranges**. There are also large areas of high, rocky land called plateaus. The Tibetan plateau is in southern China. It is higher than most mountains in the United States or Europe.

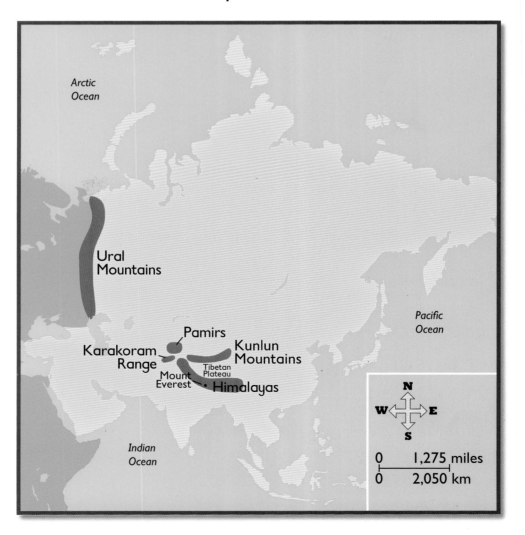

Mount Everest is the world's tallest mountain. It is the highest place on Earth.

▲ *Mount Everest is in the Himalayas, in Nepal*

The Himalayan Mountains are on the **border** between China and Nepal. Parts are also in India and Bhutan. Sir Edmund Hillary and Tenzing Norgay reached the top of Everest in 1953.

# Deserts

Much of central Asia is **desert**. The rocky Gobi Desert in China is very hot in summer and cold in winter. People called Mongols live there in circular tents. These tents are called yurts. They can be moved from place to place.

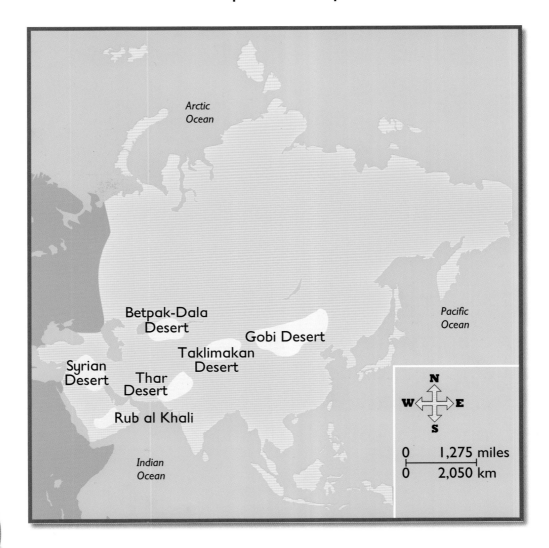

▲ *People drill for oil in Saudi Arabia.*

People drill for oil beneath the sandy deserts of southwestern Asia. Pipes carry the oil to **ports** on the coast. Large ships, called oil tankers, then take it all over the world.

# Rivers

The world's first cities were built by people living near the Tigris and Euphrates rivers. It was easy to grow food in the land there. Farmers sailed along these rivers and **traded** food for other things.

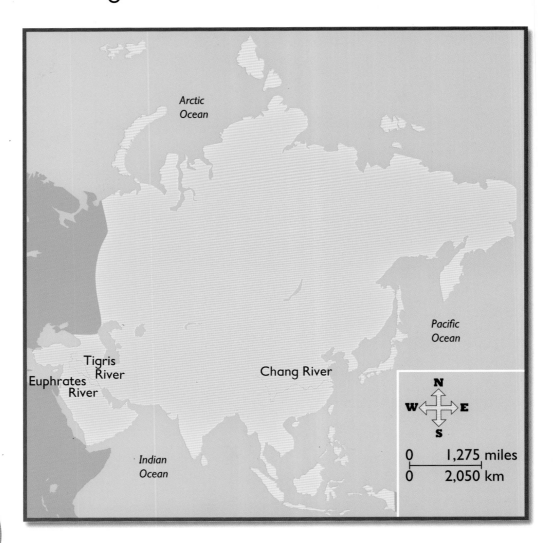

Arctic Ocean

Pacific Ocean

Tigris River

Euphrates River

Chang River

Indian Ocean

N
W E
S

0    1,275 miles
0    2,050 km

The Chang (or Yangtze) River is the third largest river in the world.

▲ *The Chang runs through China.*

The Chang (or Yangtze) River flows through China for 3,964 miles (6,380 kilometers). People have built huge **dams** on the Chang. The water rushing through these dams is used to make electricity.

# Lakes and Seas

Asia has many large lakes. The largest is called the Caspian Sea. But it is really the world's biggest **saltwater** lake.

▲ *A woman floats in the Dead Sea.*

The Dead Sea is also really a lake. It is the lowest lake on Earth. The water in the Dead Sea is so salty that people can float in it very easily. It lies between Israel and Jordan.

# Plants

Farmers grow rice all over southern Asia. They plant the rice in flooded fields called rice paddies. The islands of Southeast Asia are famous for their spices, such as nutmeg, pepper, and cloves.

Asian farmers grow most of the world's rice, rubber, cotton, and tea.

▲ *Rice paddies grow in Indonesia*

Bamboo is actually a very fast growing grass.

▲ *Indonesia has many bamboo plants.*

Bamboo grows as tall as trees in the forests of China and Southeast Asia. People use the woody bamboo stems to make houses, fishing poles, and **rafts**.

# Animals

Giant pandas live in southwest China. It feeds almost entirely on bamboo shoots. The Chinese government has set aside special areas of forest where giant pandas can live safely.

Fewer than 1,000 giant pandas now live in the wild.

▲ *This giant panda lives in China*

▲ *This orangutan lives in Borneo*

The orangutan is also very rare. This giant ape now only lives in the **rain forests** on the islands of Borneo and Sumatra. People are trying to protect the rain forests and the amazing creatures that live there.

# Languages

This map shows the names of some of the countries of Asia. The people of Asia speak many different languages. In India there are 16 **official** languages. But in southwest Asia many people speak Arabic.

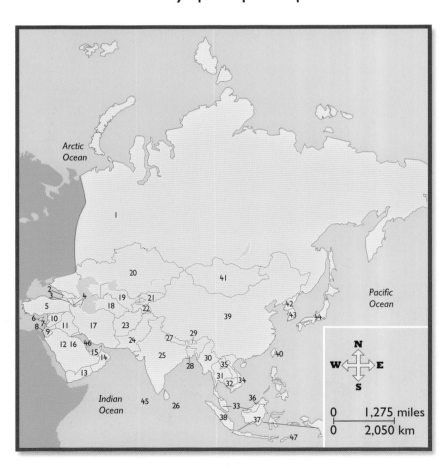

| | |
|---|---|
| 1. Russia | 24. Pakistan |
| 2. Georgia | 25. India |
| 3. Armenia | 26. Sri Lanka |
| 4. Azerbaijan | 27. Nepal |
| 5. Turkey | 28. Bangladesh |
| 6. Cyprus | 29. Bhutan |
| 7. Lebanon | 30. Myanmar |
| 8. Israel | 31. Thailand |
| 9. Jordan | 32. Cambodia |
| 10. Syria | 33. Malaysia |
| 11. Iraq | 34. Vietnam |
| 12. Saudi Arabia | 35. Laos |
| 13. Yemen | 36. Brunei |
| 14. Oman | 37. Indonesia |
| 15. United Arab Emirates | 38. Sumatra |
| 16. Kuwait | 39. China |
| 17. Iran | 40. Taiwan |
| 18. Turkmenistan | 41. Mongolia |
| 19. Uzbekistan | 42. North Korea |
| 20. Kazakstan | 43. South Korea |
| 21. Kyrgyzstan | 44. Japan |
| 22. Tajikistan | 45. Maldives |
| 23. Afghanistan | 46. Bahrain |
| | 47. East Timor |

Children in China have to learn thousands of symbols before they can read and write.

▲ *A girl in China learns how to write.*

Many Asian languages have their own alphabets that are used for writing. Other languages have a different symbol for each word. Some Asian writing is read from right to left. Other writing is read from top to bottom.

# Cities

Asia has some of the world's biggest cities. Mumbai, in India, is a huge, crowded city. It was built on an island 700 years ago. Mumbai used to be called Bombay. It is famous for its Bollywood film studios. Tokyo is another huge city. It is in Japan.

More people live in Tokyo than in any other city in the world.

▲ *Tokyo is a busy city.*

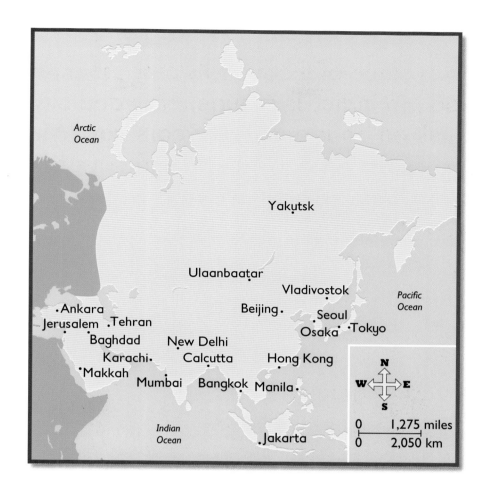

This map shows some of the most important cities in Asia. Makkah, in Saudi Arabia, is an important place for **Muslims**. It is where the **prophet** Mohammed was born. Mohammed started the Muslim religion.

# In the Country

People, called Bedouins, live in the **deserts** of western Asia. They sleep in tents and roam through the deserts. They look for places where their animals can eat. Their camels can survive for a long time without drinking water.

▲ *Bedouins live in the desert.*

▲ *This floating market is in Thailand.*

Many Asian farmers live in small villages close to their farms. Some farmers take their **crops** to floating markets. People come to the banks (sides) of the river and buy food from the boats.

# Famous Places

The Forbidden City is a huge walled palace inside the city of Beijing, China. It was built by Chinese **emperors** 600 years ago. For 500 years, only the emperor's family and servants were allowed to enter the palace.

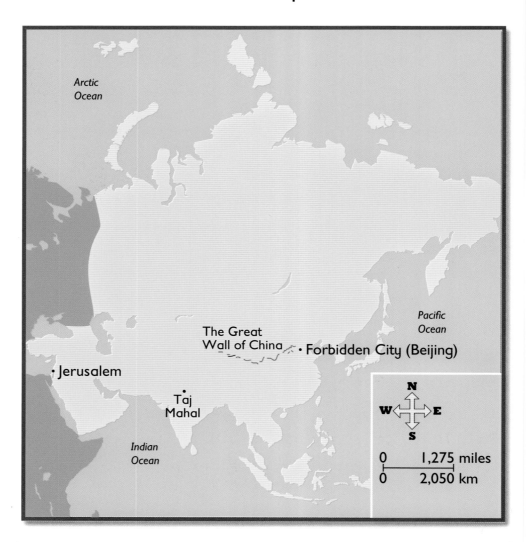

Arctic Ocean

Pacific Ocean

The Great Wall of China • Forbidden City (Beijing)

• Jerusalem

• Taj Mahal

Indian Ocean

N
W E
S

0        1,275 miles
0        2,050 km

The Great Wall of China is so big it can be seen from space.

▲ *The Great Wall of China is very long.*

The Great Wall of China stretches for 1,400 miles (2,250 kilometres). It was built by the first emperor of China over 2,000 years ago to keep northern warriors out. When soldiers saw an enemy, they lit a fire in their watchtower.

Jerusalem is a holy city for Jews, Christians, and Muslims.

▲ *Jerusalem is in Israel.*

Inside Jerusalem, Israel, is part of a temple built by a **Jewish** king over 2,000 years ago. Jerusalem also contains the **Christian** Church of the Holy Sepulcher, and the **Muslim** Dome of the Rock. They are all important religious buildings.

The Taj Mahal is a beautiful **tomb** made from white **marble**. A Muslim ruler built it for his wife.

The Taj Mahal took 22 years to complete.

▲ *The Taj Mahal is in India.*

# Fast Facts

## Asia's longest rivers

| Name of river | Length in miles | Length in kilometers | Countries | Sea it flows into |
|---|---|---|---|---|
| Yangtze/ Chang | 3,964 | 6,380 | China | East China Sea |
| Yenisey–Angara | 3,449 | 5,550 | Russia, Mongolia | Kara Sea |
| Huang He (Yellow) | 3,395 | 5,463 | China | Bohai Sea |

## Asia's highest mountains

| Name of mountain | Height in metres | Height in feet | Country or region |
|---|---|---|---|
| Everest | 8,850 | 29,035 | Nepal/Tibet |
| K–2 | 8,611 | 28,250 | Kashmir |
| Kanchenjunga | 8,598 | 28,208 | Nepal/India |

## Asia's record breakers

Over three billion people live in Asia. That is more than in any other continent.

China has more people than any other country in the world. China's biggest city, Shanghai, has 13.3 million people.

Asia has part of the largest country in the world: Russia. The rest of Russia is in Europe.

Asia has the lowest place on Earth. The Dead Sea is 1,293 feet (394 meters) below sea level.

All the world's major religions started in Asia, including Judaism (the **Jewish** religion), Islam, Christianity, Buddhism, Sikhism, and Hinduism.

# Glossary

**Arctic Circle** imaginary line that circles Earth near the North Pole

**border** dividing line between one country and another

**Christian** someone who follows Christianity, the religion based on the teachings of Jesus Christ

**climate** type of weather a place has

**crop** plant that is grown for food

**dam** wall built across a river to control the water

**desert** hot, dry area with very little rain

**emperor** ruler of an empire

**Equator** imaginary circle around the exact middle of Earth

**Jewish** describes someone who follows Judaism, the religion based on the laws of Moses

**marble** hard stone that can be polished and used in buildings and statues

**Muslim** someone who follows the religion of Islam, taught by the prophet Mohammed

**official** approved by the government

**port** place where ships come and go

**prophet** someone who tells about things that will happen in the future

**raft** simple platform used to move people or things over water

**rain forest** thick forest that has heavy rain all year round

**range** line of mountains that are connected to each other

**saltwater** water that is salty, like the sea

**tomb** house or room where a dead person is buried

**trade** buy or sell things

# More Books to Read

Lynch, Emma. *We're from China*. Chicago: Heinemann Library, 2005.

Parker, Vic. *We're from India*. Chicago: Heinemann Library, 2005.

Underwood, Deborah. *Watching Orangutans in Asia*. Chicago: Heinemann Library, 2006.

# Index